Fruit Salad

by Althea
pictures by Jacqueline Wood

Published by Dinosaur Publications

Do you like fruit salad?

The fruit we eat is full of natural sugar and gives us some of the vitamins we need to keep us healthy.

We eat it fresh or drink the juices from it. We also buy fruit frozen, tinned, dried or made into jam.

But how does all the fruit grow?

apple bud

blossom

Cut the apple in half and find the pips.

fruit

nectarine

peach

In the middle of each fruit there is a single stone, which may grow into a tree.

Some plums are dried. This changes them into prunes.

Strawberry plants grow close to the ground. The straw helps to keep them clean.

Raspberries and blackberries grow on bushes.
When picking wild blackberries growing in hedges, you will find the plant is very prickly.

Blackcurrant juice is good to drink.

blackcurrant

gooseberry

redcurrant

All these soft fruits
make lovely jam and jelly
so long as you can stop
the birds from eating them first!

blueberry

Citrus fruits grow in warm countries.
They are packed and sent overseas
in ships and aeroplanes.
Their thick skins protect
them from damage on the journey.

mandarin

grapefruit   lemon   satsuma

The Romans were probably the first people to grow grapes and figs in England.
Grapes grow on vines.
Some will be dried to change them into raisins and currants.
Grapes are also used to make wine.

raisins

The fig grows its flowers inside the fruit. For the seed to grow, the fig wasp has to crawl in through a small hole to pollinate the flowers.

water melon

There are many different sorts of melon.
They need a lot of water to make them grow.

The plants are grown from the seeds found inside the melon. They will take three to four months to grow.

cantaloupe

honeydew

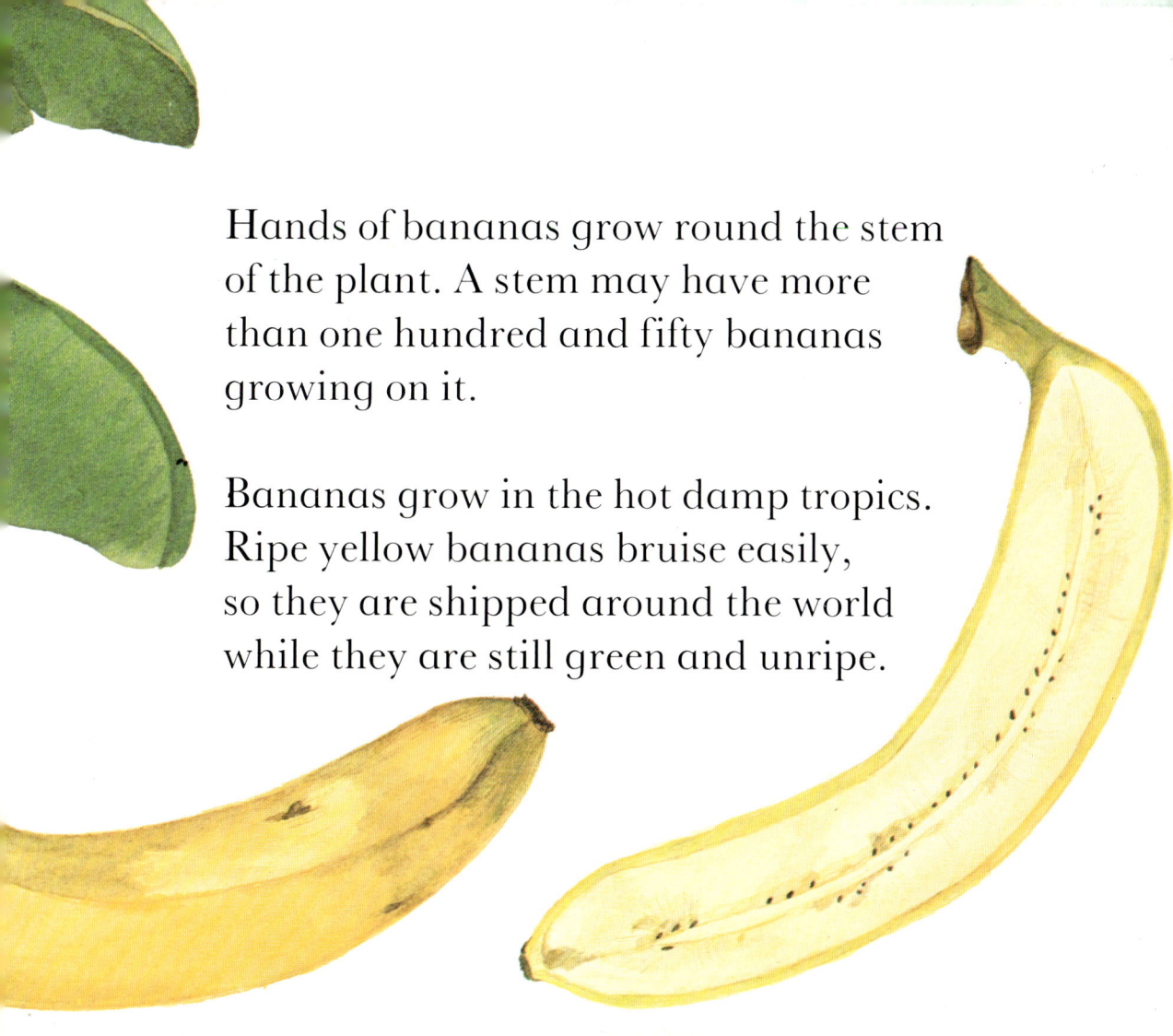

Hands of bananas grow round the stem of the plant. A stem may have more than one hundred and fifty bananas growing on it.

Bananas grow in the hot damp tropics. Ripe yellow bananas bruise easily, so they are shipped around the world while they are still green and unripe.

Pineapples also grow in the tropics.
They were first found in South America.
The plants have sharp spiny leaves.
Pineapples can be grown by planting
the crown of leaves cut from the top
of the fruit.

The fruit is often chopped
or sliced and put into tins.

Look out for these other fruits which also grow in warm climates.

pomegranate

passion fruit

mango

persimmon   lychee   kumquat   kiwi fruit

You can try to grow plants from the stone, pips or seeds you find inside your fruit.

Text copyright © Althea Braithwaite 1987
Illustrations copyright © Jacqueline Wood 1987
Published by Dinosaur Publications
8 Grafton Street, London W1X 3LA

Dinosaur Publications is an imprint of Fontana Paperbacks, part of the Collins Publishing Group

Printed by Warners of Bourne and London